THE FACTS ABOUT
Epilepsy

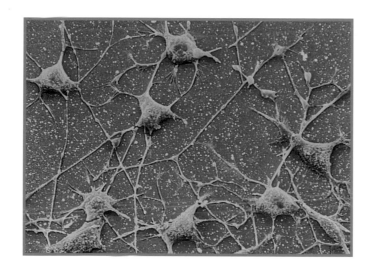

Claire Llewellyn

Thameside Press

Distributed in the United States by
Smart Apple Media
1980 Lookout Drive
North Mankato, MN 56003

Text by Claire Llewellyn
Illustration by Tom Connell

Editor: Russell McLean
Designer: Helen James
Picture researcher: Frances Vargo
Medical consultant: Lynn Clack, Roald Dahl Sapphire Nurse (Epilepsy), Addenbrooke's
    NHS Trust, Cambridge, England

Thanks to Ann Scherer, Epilepsy Foundation of America, for help with the U.S. edition.

Printed in China

9 8 7 6 5 4 3 2 1

Library of Congress Cataloging-in-Publication Data

Llewellyn, Claire.
    Epilepsy / written by Claire Llewellyn.
        p. cm. -- (The facts about ...)
    Includes index.
    ISBN 1-929298-96-X
        1. Epilepsy--Juvenile literature. 2. Epilepsy in children--Juvenile literature. [1.
    Epilepsy. 2. Diseases.] I. Title. II. Facts about (Mankato, Minn.)

    RC372.2 .L565 2001
    616.8'53--dc21

                                                                    2001023424

Picture acknowledgements:
Addenbrooke's NHS Trust: Greg Harding 23t & b. Corbis: Archivo Iconografico, S.A. 27t;
Doug Wilson 29t. Eye Ubiquitous: J. Burke 5b. Sally & Richard Greenhill: Sally Greenhill 25t
& b; Richard Greenhill 28b. MedicAlert: 15t. Medipics: MIG cover bc, 18b. Photofusion: Mark
Campbell 3r, 16b; Colin Edwards 11b, 17t; Gina Glover 27b; Crispin Hughes 9b; Ute Klapnake
cover background, 4t; Clarissa Leahy 16t; Julia Martin 3l, 17b, 20b, 29b; G. Montgomery 15b;
Peter Olive 26t; Liz Somerville 11t; Martin Wilson 13t. Rex Features: Chat Magazine 14b.
Robert Harding Picture Library: 5t, 9t, 21b; C. Bowman 4b; Martyn Chillmaid cover br, 10t,
12t; N. Penny/MR 13b; S. Villeger/Explorer: 22. Science Photo Library: BSIP VEM 3c, 19b; BSIP
Laurent/H. Americain 28t; Conor Caffrey 14t, 26b; CNRI cover bl, 07b; Custom Medical Stock
Photo 6b; Gaillard Jerrican 21t; Maximilian Stock Ltd 19t; Joseph Nettis 8b; Chris Priest 7t;
Quest 1, 6t; SAADA/EUROLIOS 8t; Saturn Stills 18t. David Towersey: 10b, 20t, 24t & b.

Contents

Words in **bold** are explained
in the glossary on page 30

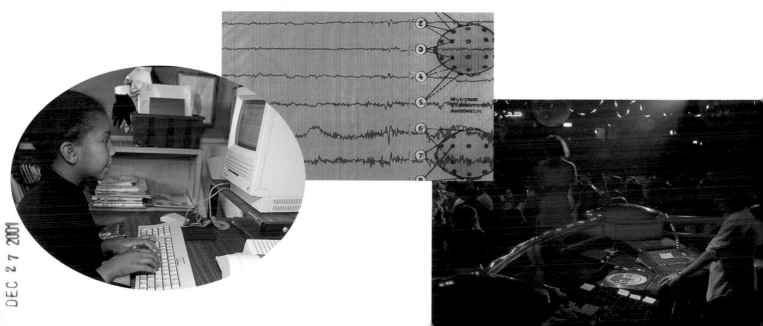

What is epilepsy?

Epilepsy is a condition that affects the brain. We rely on our brains to keep our bodies working properly. But, with epilepsy, messages passing to and from the brain sometimes become confused. This can make people behave in unusual ways.

Epilepsy only affects people at some times.

The signs of epilepsy

Most of the time, there are no signs that someone has epilepsy. But sometimes they will start to feel strange and their behavior may suddenly change.

They may sweat, tremble, and seem confused. Or, quite suddenly, they may **black out**, fall down, and start to shake. This is known as a **seizure**. It usually lasts for a minute or two.

Having a seizure

Many people live with epilepsy. For each person, a seizure feels slightly different, and their body behaves in different ways. Some people become **unconscious** and remember little or nothing at all. Others can describe their seizures.

Epilepsy often starts early in life.

Did you know?

- A seizure is sometimes called a convulsion, a spell, an attack, or a dizzy. A "good day" may mean few seizures.
- African Americans sometimes call a seizure "falling out."
- The word epilepsy comes from a Greek word meaning "to seize" or "to attack."

There are no outward signs that someone has epilepsy.

"When you have a seizure, it's like you're in a weird place and you hear voices shouting your name and your head keeps going round in circles."

SIAN, AGE 11

Many young people have epilepsy. It doesn't have to rule their lives.

Living with epilepsy

Epilepsy can range from mild to severe. For many people, especially children, it is easily controlled so that seizures are rare. In time, their seizures may even stop completely. Other people need medicines all their lives. For them, seizures are a way of life. A few people have such severe epilepsy that it affects their learning and every aspect of their life. They need life-long treatment and support.

"It's like when you're watching TV, and the picture gets blurry and fuzzy for a minute and then goes back on again okay."

PETER, AGE 9

Explaining epilepsy

The brain is the world's most complicated machine. Amazingly, it works without a hitch most of the time. But if a person has epilepsy, the brain can lose control briefly and cause an epileptic seizure.

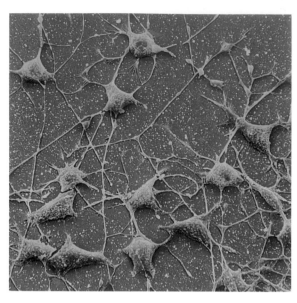

A microscope shows a network of nerve cells. Nerve signals pass between them.

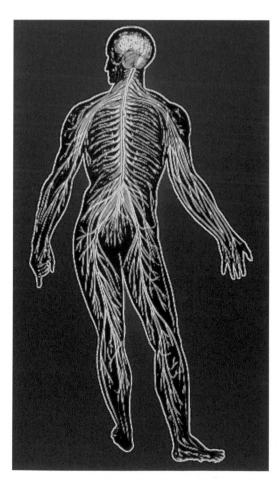

The **nervous system** carries messages to every part of the body.

The brain

The brain is the body's control center. It contains many millions of **nerve cells,** all connected to one another. When the brain is working properly, the nerve cells buzz with activity. They receive signals from the rest of the body, send out messages, and keep every part of the body under control.

Wrong messages

When someone has epilepsy, nerve cells in one part of the brain may lose control briefly. The signals are **disrupted** and the cells pass the wrong messages.

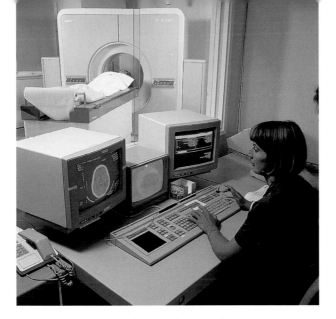

A scanning machine shows the inner workings of the brain.

This can affect nearby nerve cells, too, so that the disturbance spreads to other parts of the brain. This disorganized activity causes a seizure. What a person feels when they have a seizure and how it looks to an outsider depends on where the trouble begins in the brain, and how widely and quickly it spreads.

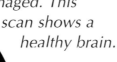

A scan can show whether a part of the brain has been damaged. This scan shows a healthy brain.

Types of seizure

There are two main types of epileptic seizure. A **generalized seizure** involves the whole brain; a **partial seizure** affects just one part of the brain. Often what starts as a partial seizure spreads to become a generalized seizure. The effects of a seizure can vary greatly. Some seizures cause unusual or distressing behavior. Others are slight and are over so quickly that no one would notice them. In most cases, they last a couple of minutes. Then the nerve cells return to normal.

Who has epilepsy?

The reasons why someone develops epilepsy are not always clear. The condition affects people of all races and abilities. It appears most often in younger people, but older people develop it, too.

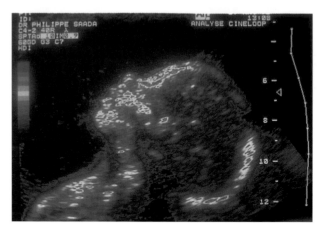

A scan checks that a baby's brain is developing properly before it is born.

Causes of epilepsy

There are many reasons why someone may develop epilepsy. Sometimes the cause is obvious. Perhaps a baby's brain has not developed properly before birth, or has been damaged during a difficult birth.

A brain infection, such as **meningitis**, or a head injury can also cause epilepsy. Epilepsy may also be the sign of a brain tumor. Older people sometimes develop the condition after a **heart attack** or a **stroke**.

A family connection

In most cases of epilepsy (70 per cent), there is no obvious cause. Often there is a family connection, with more than one member of a family having epilepsy.

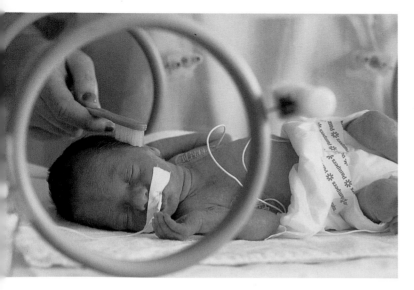

About a third of all new cases of epilepsy are babies or children.

*About half of all epilepsy
starts before age 25.*

Did you know?

- In the U.S., about one in 100 children has epilepsy. That's about 2 or 3 in every elementary school.
- Out of every ten children with epilepsy, three or four will grow out of it when they are teenagers.
- About 2.3 million people in the U.S. have epilepsy.
- Epilepsy even affects animals.

Children with epilepsy

Epilepsy usually appears in children and teenagers. At this age the brain is still developing, and is more likely to have seizures. Having epilepsy as a child does not always mean you will have it for life. Medicines can control the condition so well that the seizures may stop. But the epilepsy itself is not cured, and the seizures may return.

Older people

Older people are more likely to have strokes or heart attacks, which may damage the brain. Seizures can be harder to deal with in later life, and their effects can be long-lasting.

Falling during a seizure can cause injuries to older, **brittle** bones. And because older people often live alone, there may be no one to lend a hand.

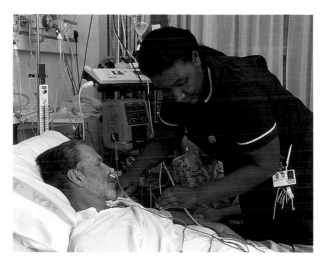

Epilepsy sometimes follows a heart attack.

Having a seizure

During a generalized seizure, the whole brain is briefly "out of order." The person may fall to the ground and twitch and jerk. In other types of generalized seizure, there is nothing to see.

A seizure can leave you feeling very tired.

A seizure step-by-step
What happens when someone has a generalized seizure? An onlooker may see some of the following signs:

1 Without warning, the person may lose consciousness and fall to the ground. They may cry out as air is squeezed out of the lungs, but they are not in any pain.

2 All the **muscles** in the body begin to tighten and relax, tighten and relax, over and over again. This makes the body twitch and jerk.

3 The person's face turns pale or even a little blue, and they may bite their tongue or dribble. **Saliva** may make bubbles around the mouth. Their breathing may sound noisy, and because all their muscles have relaxed, they may wet their pants. They can't help this, as the seizure makes it happen.

A person is not in pain during a seizure.

Children who have lots of absence seizures sometimes find it hard to keep up at school.

4 As they come out of the seizure, people often have little idea about what has happened or even where they are. They may feel tired and have a headache and may need to sleep. Because their muscles have been working so hard, they may feel a few aches and pains over the next couple of days.

Did you know?

- A major generalized seizure is also called a **tonic-clonic seizure** or a grand mal.
- Some seizures are just muscle jerks, like the ones you sometimes have when falling asleep.

"When I have a seizure I go a bit stiff, fall over and my body shakes. They last about three minutes. I rest for a bit and then carry on doing what I was doing before."
SIMON, AGE 10

Absence seizures

An **absence seizure** is a different type of generalized seizure. The person looks blank and seems to be day-dreaming, but cannot hear or see anything around them. This lasts for only a second or two. Although the seizures are short and slight, they can have serious effects. Some children have hundreds every day, which may affect their learning.

Other generalized seizures

There are other kinds of generalized seizures. Sometimes, instead of going stiff, a person's body goes floppy and collapses to the floor. They do not twitch or jerk, but are still unconscious throughout.

An absence seizure may be no more than a moment's blankness.

Partial seizures

When someone has a partial seizure, only one part of the brain is disturbed. In some of these seizures, the person is fully conscious; in others they are not.

Parts of the brain

Different parts of the brain control all the different things we can do. One part controls movement, while others control touch, speech, sight, hearing, speaking, and thinking.

A person may be fully aware during a partial seizure.

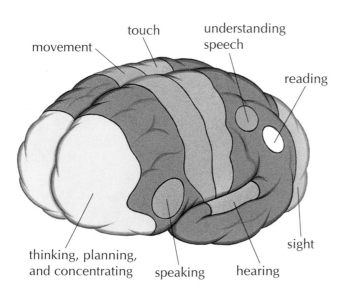

Certain parts of the brain, known as centers, control the different things we can do.

Strange feelings

Any of these skills may be affected during a partial seizure. A person's arm may start to twitch or they may feel a tingling in the leg. They may be aware of a strange smell, taste, or noise. Their hearing or sight may be disturbed and things may look too large or too small. Often the person is fully aware, yet has no way of controlling or stopping the seizure. It simply has to run its course.

Some people feel irritable or tired several days before a seizure.

Unusual behavior

In other kinds of partial seizure people are unaware of where they are or what they are doing. They may fumble with their buttons, pluck at their clothes, or begin to take them off. People can feel sad, happy, lonely, or afraid during a partial seizure. The problem with this kind of seizure is that onlookers may not realize it is even taking place, and may be confused by the person's behavior.

Certain types of seizure are more likely during sleep.

Auras and warnings

People who have partial seizures nearly always have some kind of warning, or **aura**—a feeling which tells them a seizure has begun. This may be a slight dizziness, a feeling of pins and needles, a movement in their thumb, or a tiny twitch on their face. Some people feel different a few days before a seizure—perhaps restless, irritable, or tired. These signs are often noticed by people who are close to them.

"Once, at school, it came over me during a race. I stood there staring and then the race finished. Every day my day-dreaming became longer... My brothers used to hit me on the back to bring me back to reality."

JONATHAN, AGE 10

A helping hand

Seeing a seizure for the first time can be scary. But if you understand what is happening, you are much more likely to be able to give someone a helping hand.

Feeling confident

The most important thing to do if someone has a seizure is to stay calm. Understanding epilepsy and knowing how to help will make you, and everyone else, feel more confident.

Do your best to reassure someone after a seizure.

Remember that there is nothing you can do to stop or shorten a seizure. You must allow it to run its course.

Don't...

- Try to hold the person.
- Try to move the person, unless they are in a dangerous place.
- Put anything in their mouth.
- Give anything to eat or drink.

When the seizure is over, place the person on their side to recover.

Carrying I.D.

Many people with epilepsy wear a bracelet or necklace with a small medal naming the condition. Some also carry I.D. cards with first-aid instructions. If they have a seizure, an onlooker can help.

If you have seizures, it can be useful to wear an identity bracelet.

Do...
- Stay calm.
- Stay with the person.
- Put something soft under their head.
- Move anything that could hurt them.
- Stop other people crowding round.

Afterwards...
- Put the person on their side. This helps their breathing and allows any saliva to drain away.
- Tell the person where they are and what has happened.
- Reassure the person and try to prevent them feeling embarrassed.

"When I was at elementary school, I had a bad seizure. My friends were very scared and didn't know what to do. But now I have Clare, Sarah, Becky, Rachel, and Anna who I can rely on when I don't feel well.'

ALISON, AGE 12

Call an ambulance (911)...
- If a seizure lasts longer than five minutes.
- If a second seizure quickly follows the first.
- If the person is having trouble breathing after the seizure.
- If the person is badly hurt.
- If the person has never had a seizure before.

Always call an ambulance if one seizure follows another.

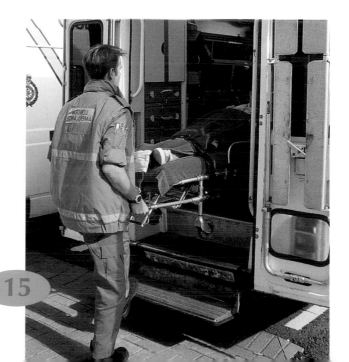

What brings on a seizure?

Most people with epilepsy never know when they are going to have a seizure. Others can pinpoint certain things that seem to spark off their seizures. These are known as **triggers**.

Types of trigger

Seizures do not always come out of the blue. They are sometimes linked to what a person is doing, but are also caused by thoughts and feelings.

Some people with epilepsy find they have seizures when they are feeling tired.

For some people, disco lights can spark off a seizure.

Sometimes a trigger can be very specific. It may be a certain movement or thought, or something seen or heard. Once someone has discovered a trigger, they may be able to cut down their seizures by avoiding it.

Illness

A seizure is more likely when someone is feeling under the weather, even if they only have a mild cold. Eating plenty of fresh fruit and vegetables helps to fight off infections.

Flickering sunlight can trigger seizures. Sunglasses help to prevent this.

Flickering lights

Some people are **photosensitive**. In other words, they are especially sensitive to flickering lights. Disco lights, flickering sunlight, and television or computer screens are common triggers for them. It helps to avoid discos, watch television from a good distance in a well-lit room, and wear sunglasses on a sunny day.

Lack of sleep

Tiredness can bring on a seizure—whether it is caused by too many late nights, **jet lag**, or working night shifts. For most people, a late night now and again is not a problem, but it helps to have regular sleep patterns and to catch up quickly on lost sleep.

Hunger

Skipping breakfast or going for too long between meals can trigger seizures. People with epilepsy need to eat regular meals.

Feelings and stress

Some people have seizures when they are feeling anxious, excited, angry, sad, or maybe even guilty. We cannot avoid these feelings, but finding ways to understand and cope with them can be very useful. Learning to relax is helpful.

Be happy!

Being happy is one of the best ways of cutting down seizures. Children with epilepsy have fewer seizures when they are enjoying themseves. This is also true of adults.

Having fun is a good way to avoid seizures.

Finding out about epilepsy

When someone has a seizure for the first time, they need to see a doctor. The doctor may send them for some tests. These help the doctor to identify their condition. In other words, he or she makes a **diagnosis**.

A doctor listens carefully as a patient describes her seizure.

At the doctor's

Epilepsy is not the only reason why someone may behave strangely or lose consciousness. So, before making a diagnosis, the doctor needs to know exactly what happened during the seizure. They ask the patient and any friends who saw the seizure to describe it in detail.

At the hospital

If the doctor suspects epilepsy, the patient is usually sent to the hospital to see a **specialist neurologist—** a doctor who is an expert on the brain. The specialist carries out some tests to discover what caused the seizure. The first and most important test is called an **electroencephalogram,** or EEG for short.

Someone who has an EEG is asked to open and close their eyes, breathe deeply, and look at a flashing light.

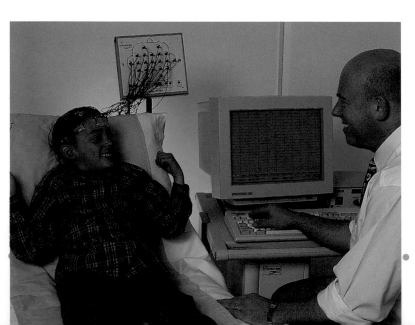

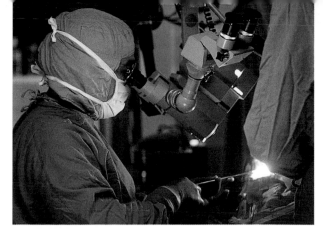

Lasers are used in some operations to treat epilepsy. They do not even leave a scar.

"Today I'm going for my EEG to see how many fits I'm having. I've had one before and was scared because I didn't know why they were putting things on my head, but today I'm not frightened."

CLAIRE, AGE 10

Tests for epilepsy

An EEG takes less than an hour and is completely painless. Small disks or pads called **electrodes** are fixed on the head to record electrical activity in the brain. The EEG picks up any unusual brain activity and can help to identify if the person is having generalized or partial seizures. If the specialist needs more information, they may order a brain scan. Scans provide x-rays and other detailed pictures of the brain, which may show damage.

The results

All this information helps a doctor to have a fuller picture of a patient's condition. Understanding the type of seizure a person is having affects their treatment. A few people can have an operation to remove the damaged part of the brain. But most people will need medicines to control their epilepsy in the future.

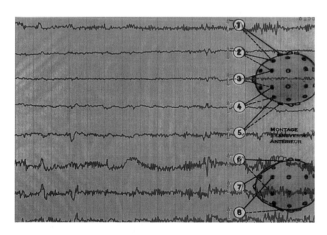

The result of an EEG reveals activity in different parts of the brain.

Did you know?

- Panic attacks, headaches, heart disease, or a high temperature are some of the causes of seizures, besides epilepsy.
- Someone who has seizures only when they are tired may have an EEG while they sleep.
- In the U.S., about one in ten people has a seizure at some time in their life, but this does not always lead to epilepsy.

Controlling epilepsy

Four out of five people with epilepsy can control their seizures with medicine. These medicines are known as **antiepileptic** drugs. They can allow people to lead a normal life. Some people need an operation, if the medicines don't help.

Antiepileptic drugs help to control seizures. Some people take them for life.

Calming the brain

Antiepileptic drugs work by calming the brain cells when they start to lose control. The drugs are introduced gradually so that they build up in the body quite slowly.

Some drugs may cause **side effects**, such as sleepiness or a rash. Doctors try to give the lowest possible **dose** of a drug which will control the seizures without causing unwanted side effects. Some people with epilepsy, especially children, eat a special diet. Seizures can also be controlled by putting a small battery into a person's chest. This is called vagus nerve stimulation (VNS).

Eating regular meals is one way to help control epilepsy.

Five ways to help control epilepsy

1 Take your medicine regularly.
2 Find out what triggers the epilepsy, and learn to avoid it.
3 Eat regular meals.
4 Have a regular bedtime.
5 Pace yourself, giving time to work, rest, and play.

Keeping a seizure diary is important. It may help to identify certain triggers.

Remember, remember!

Most antiepileptic medicines have to be taken two or three times a day. A good way of remembering to take the tablets is to keep them in a pill box. The box contains a tray for each day of the week, with a compartment for each dose.

Drugs allow most people with epilepsy to live a normal life.

Keeping a diary

Many people keep a seizure diary to help them control their epilepsy. They jot down the date and details of any seizures, and any possible triggers. The diary gives the doctor a useful picture and shows if the drugs are working. If someone has had no seizures for a couple of years, the doctor may decide to reduce their dose. In time, they may not need drugs at all. But someone with epilepsy must never alter the dose on their own, as a sudden change can bring on seizures.

"Keeping a diary for six months showed I was more likely to have a seizure when I had gone without sleep."
ZOE, AGE 11

Epilepsy nurses

Epilepsy nurses work alongside doctors, offering help and advice to patients, parents, and anyone else who is touched by epilepsy.

Epilepsy nurses are specially trained to help people of all ages who have epilepsy.

What does a nurse do?
Many people are involved in the care of a child with epilepsy—relatives, the family doctor, the specialist, and teachers. An epilepsy nurse is a link between them all, giving advice, information, and help.

In the hospital
Most epilepsy nurses are based in the outpatient department of a hospital. This is where people with epilepsy come to have tests or to see the specialist. The nurse explains the tests, helps to carry them out, chases the results, and explains the diagnosis.

Sometimes people with epilepsy need to stay in the hospital, perhaps because they are having more seizures. The nurse spends time with them on the ward.

At home

When a child is diagnosed with epilepsy, parents often need help to understand the condition and plan for the future. They may need advice in planning a vacation, for example, or they may have concerns about school. The nurse talks over these issues with the parents, and helps them solve any problems. She visits people in their homes after school or in the evening so that she can see the whole family.

Epilepsy nurses spend a lot of time on the phone. Many people ring them for advice.

At school

The Epilepsy Foundation of America encourages school nurses to give general talks to teachers and other staff about the causes of epilepsy and what to do during a seizure. Nurses also discuss the importance of supporting children with epilepsy so that they get the most out of school.

Explaining epilepsy to children and their parents is part of a nurse's job.

Daily life

Most people with epilepsy enjoy full and active lives. They do not need special treatment. But there is always the risk of an unexpected seizure, and so it makes sense to take extra care at home.

Trailing cords could be a danger in the event of a seizure.

In the bathroom

Take showers rather than baths if possible. A bath should always be run with cold water first, to avoid the risk of **scalding**. Keep the water shallow. Do not lock the bathroom door—use an occupied sign instead.

Avoid the risk of having a seizure in the tub by taking showers instead.

In the kitchen

If someone has a seizure in the kitchen, a stove can cause serious burns. Using a microwave oven is safer. If an ordinary stove is used, cook on the burners at the back and fit a guard rail at the front.

In the living room

Avoid open fires in the living room, or use a fireguard. To help prevent injury in a fall, fit safety glass in doors and windows, and have soft carpets if possible. Avoid long, trailing cords, which could pull out or snag in a fall.

Cycling is good exercise—but keep away from busy roads and wear a helmet.

Sport and exercise

Exercise is good for everyone. If you have epilepsy, swimming is fine as long as you take a few sensible precautions.

- Don't swim alone.
- Don't swim if you are feeling tired or unwell.
- Make sure a companion knows about your epilepsy and what to do in a seizure.
- Stay in fairly shallow water.
- Don't swim in rivers or the sea.
- At swimming pools, always tell a lifeguard about your epilepsy.
- Avoid diving from the high board.

"When I first took the medicine I was not allowed to swim without my mum or dad watching me. It was in case I fainted. Now I am in the school swimming team."

HELEN, AGE 10

On the road

Cycling is fine for most children with epilepsy. They should always wear a helmet and stay on paths or quiet roads.

Unsuitable sports

Sports where a seizure could cause serious injury should be avoided by people with epilepsy. These include diving, parachuting, hang-gliding, and mountaineering.

Few people have seizures when they are having fun in the swimming pool.

Talking about epilepsy

People who have epilepsy are not ill. Seizures are only a tiny part of their life. In between, most of them are the same as everybody else. So why do many people find their epilepsy embarrassing? And what can other people do to help?

Most children with epilepsy can do anything anyone else can do.

Other people's attitudes

Epilepsy is one of the oldest and most misunderstood medical conditions. Hundreds of years ago, people who had seizures were thought to be mad or **possessed** by the devil. They were often locked up or kept in chains.

Even today people with epilepsy are often thought of as different. They may feel uncomfortable simply because their seizures could embarrass or distress other people.

Being open

It helps to talk about epilepsy. Explaining what causes the condition and what happens during a seizure helps to tackle people's fear and ignorance. This makes everyone feel more confident.

Sometimes people with epilepsy feel ashamed of their condition. This can make them feel lonely.

Napoleon had epilepsy. He was Emperor of France in the early nineteeth century.

Don't be ashamed

If people don't want to talk about epilepsy, it seems like the condition is something shameful. This can be especially harmful for children, who may worry about having a seizure in front of their friends, or about being picked on or teased.

A normal life

The best thing for children with epilepsy is to be able to lead a normal life, playing with others, trying new things, and not always being the center of attention. Above all, they need to feel valued and have confidence in themselves.

Most people with epilepsy don't let it stop them having fun.

"My fits do not affect my life in the slightest and I still do all the naughty things I've always done."

DANIEL, AGE 8

Questions people ask

Can children have a test to see whether they will develop epilepsy? No test can predict the future. Tests on the brain are carried out only if someone's doctor thinks that they might have had a seizure.

Do I need to go to the hospital every time I have a seizure? No, it is really not necessary, although well-meaning people often call an ambulance if they see someone having a seizure. You only need to go to hospital if you have been badly injured, or if one seizure follows on after another.

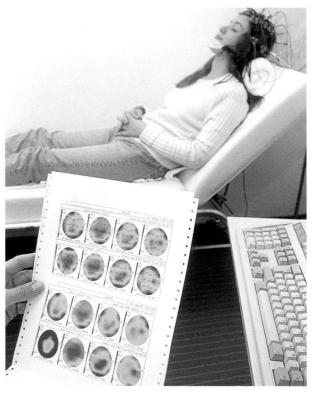

An EEG test cannot predict the future.

In some states, people with epilepsy can drive only if a doctor says they are safe.

Can I drive a car if I have epilepsy? State rules vary. You must be free of seizures for at least three months, and sometimes a year.

Should I wear a bracelet saying I have epilepsy? Wearing a bracelet is useful because people can help you if you have a seizure. Some people prefer to carry an epilepsy card in their wallet or purse.

Someone told me I couldn't be a pilot if I had epilepsy. Is that true?
You are not likely to pass the health screen to be an airline pilot, interstate truck driver, fire fighter, or part of the police. You might join the armed forces if you are free of seizures and off medicine for five years. "JobTech" is an Epilepsy Foundation service to help people with epilepsy get jobs.

Could my computer screen trigger a seizure?
Only about one in 20 people with epilepsy is sensitive to computer screens and televisions. To be on the safe side, avoid using a computer in the dark and do not sit too close to the screen.

Most people with epilepsy can use a computer.

Soccer is safe for most people with epilepsy.

Can I play football with epilepsy?
Football, hockey, soccer, and other team sports are usually safe, but your doctor may advise you to avoid them if your epilepsy was caused by a head injury.

My seizures are now under control. Will I need to take antiepileptic drugs for the rest of my life?
This depends on your medical history. Most doctors want their patient to be completely free of seizures for at least two years before considering a drop in the dose. There is a risk of more seizures when drugs are stopped.

Glossary

absence seizure A brief generalized seizure in which a person looks blank and seems to be day-dreaming.

antiepileptic Designed to control the symptoms of epilepsy. Antiepileptic medicines prevent seizures.

aura A warning sign that some people have when they are about to have a seizure. For example, it may be a certain taste or smell, a strong feeling of fear or happiness, or a tiny muscle jerk.

black out To lose consciousness.

brittle Hard and easy to break.

diagnosis Discovering what type of disease a person has.

disrupted Disturbed or confused.

dose The amount of medicine a patient is given.

electrode A metal disk or pad that picks up electrical activity.

electroencephalogram (EEG) A test that records the electrical activity in the brain, which can help to identify the type of seizure a person with epilepsy is having.

generalized seizure A type of seizure that affects the whole brain.

heart attack A blockage in one of the arteries, or tubes, which supply blood to the heart. Without blood, parts of the heart muscle may stop pumping and die.

jet lag A feeling of tiredness caused by a long plane journey across several time zones.

laser A device that produces an incredibly powerful beam of light. Lasers are used in delicate surgery, such as on the eye or brain.

meningitis A disease in which the layer of tissue around the brain becomes swollen. In some cases, the damage to the brain can lead to epilepsy.

muscle A special tissue in animals and humans that is made of cells. Messages from the brain cause the muscle to shorten and become wider (contract), or lengthen and relax.

nerve cell A cell that sends messages, in the form of electrical pulses, through the brain and nerves.

nervous system The network of nerves all around the body, including the brain.

neurological To do with the brain and nervous system.

partial seizure A type of epileptic seizure that affects only one part of the brain.

photosensitive Being sensitive to light, such as the flickering light of a television screen.

possessed Being controlled by a powerful outside force.

saliva The juice in your mouth that softens food before you swallow it.

scalding A burn caused by very hot steam or liquid.

seizure Unusual behavior that happens when nerve cells in the brain lose control and pass the wrong messages.

side effect An unpleasant effect caused by taking a medicine.

specialist neurologist A doctor who is an expert on the brain and the nervous system.

stroke Damage to the brain caused by a blocked or burst artery (one of the tubes that carries blood from the heart to all parts of the body). In some cases, part of the brain may die and cause loss of movement or speech.

tonic-clonic seizure Another name for a major generalized seizure.

trigger Something that brings on an epileptic seizure.

unconscious Asleep or unaware.

Useful organizations

Here are some organizations you can contact for more information about epilepsy.

Epilepsy Foundation of America
4351 Garden City Drive
Landover, MD 20785

Tel: (800) 332 1000
www.efa.org

Epilepsy Information Service
Tel: (800) 642 0500

Epilepsy in young children at www.geocities.com has over 1,000 case stories on site, with email addresses of parents so that families can share experiences and gain support.

Index